Pocket Kakuro for Kids

First published in Great Britain in 2006 by Virgin Books
Virgin Books Ltd
Thames Wharf Studios
Rainville Road
London
W6 9HA

All puzzles copyright © Puzzler Media Ltd.
www.puzzler.co.uk 2006

All other material © Virgin Books 2006

A catalogue record for this book is available from
the British Library.

ISBN (10) 0 7535 1138 X
(13) 978 0 7535 1138 1

The paper used in this book is a natural, recyclable product made
from wood grown in sustainable forests. The manufacturing
process conforms to the regulations of the country of origin.

Typeset by Virgin Books

Printed and bound by Bookmarque Ltd.

INTRODUCTION

The word Kakuro comes from the ancient Japanese for 'Oh no, I've used the same number twice; and I've done it in pen! Now I'm going to have to start all over again; grrrrrrrrr' and was the favourite pastime of Samurai warriors in the Land of the Rising Sun.

OK, so that's a bit untrue. The not-so-exciting truth is that the puzzles originated in America in the late 1960s and were published under the unbelievably boring name of 'cross sums'. Not surprisingly, very few people were wetting themselves with excitement over these cross sums which appeared inside books of regular word puzzles, presumably to give people a break from the even more boring crosswords.

Then a Japanese businessman, who was waiting for a plane back to his homeland and was bored of his crossword, stumbled upon an innocent-looking cross sum and decided this was something people could go mad for (he was obviously on an early flight and had had very little sleep).

But he was right! He adapted the puzzles a bit and, over the years, Kakuro became so successful that a book of Kakuro puzzles was published in 1986. It was hugely popular and over 20 volumes followed. The rest, as they say in not very good magazine articles, is history.

So, how do you play Kakuro? The rules and an explanation of how to play follow this introduction, but the object of Kakuro is to make each cell (the small squares) of each row add up to the number in the grey triangle in front or above it. It's easier to see how it works if you look at an example, so turn to page 9 and all will become clear.

And before you run away screaming 'No more maths! I'm not in school now!' don't panic.

There are actually a limited number of combinations that will lead to a row's value. For example, if you have two squares and the number beside them is 17, the numbers in the squares can only be 8 or 9. Simple! And to make things even easy-peasier, you'll find a list of some common combinations on page 17.

So, go ahead, and see if you can resist the awesome addictive power of Kakuro ('Mwa ha ha...').

THE RULES

The object of Kakuro is to fill the blank squares in the grid, only using numbers between 1 and 9.

Each Kakuro puzzle is made up of cells, which either run up or down, much like a crossword clue. Each cell is made up of between 2 and 9 squares.

These cells must be filled in with numbers that add up to the number 'clue', which is found in the shaded box alongside the cell. If a number appears in the bottom half of the box it is a downwards clue; if in the top half an across clue.

No number can appear twice in a cell.

HOW TO SOLVE
A KAKURO PUZZLE

STEP ONE

It is helpful to look for cells with the fewest squares, as these tend to be the easiest to solve. In this case there are several cells with just two squares.

A good place to start is on the right-hand side where there are two cells together with just two squares. These are marked with question marks below:

The cell running across, which must add up to **4**, can only contain 1 and 3 as no cell can have the same number twice.

The downwards cell that it joins adds up to **3**, which means the only possible combination is 1 and 2.

This therefore means that we know that the 1 must appear on both the **3** down cell and the **4** across cell. The puzzle now looks like this:

STEP TWO

There is now a 2 on the cell running across marked with **10**.

Two squares to the left of this 2 there is a downwards cell that is marked with **3**.

Because we can't have the same number on that line, and the only combination for 3 is 2+1, we can deduce that this square must be filled with a 1.

The across cell beneath it, also marked with **3**, must therefore be filled in with a 2 then a 1, as below:

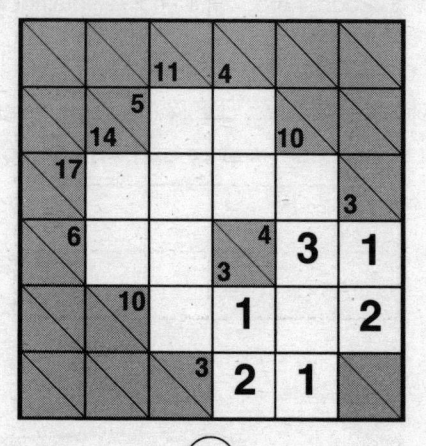

STEP THREE

We now have a 1 and a 2 on the **10** across cell. This means that the remaining squares must add up to 7.

In this case 7 has three possible combinations: 5+2, 1+6 and 3+4. As there is already a 1 and a 2 in the cell, the only possible combination is 3+4

As the blank square between the 1 and the 2 is also on another cell (the **10** down cell), which already contains a 3, we know that this is where the 4 must go and can add the 3 to the final remaining square.

With the **10** across line now filled, we can also complete the **10** down clue (3+1+4=8, therefore the last blank square must be a 2). As on page 13:

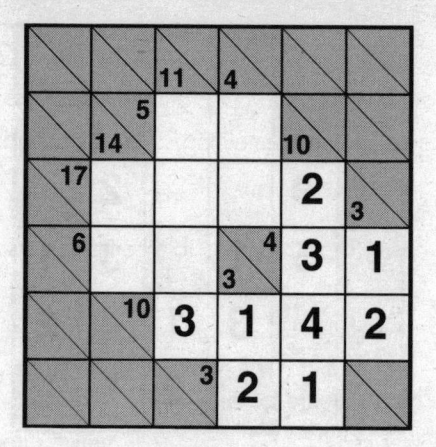

STEP FOUR

On the left-hand side of the puzzle is another pair of cells that have two spaces, one marked **14** going down and one marked **6** going across.

The only combinations for **14** are 8+6 and 9+5. However, as the cell below must add up to **6**, the only legal move is 9+5 running downwards, as all the other numbers would make the sum too high. This makes the **6** across cell 5+1 as on page 14:

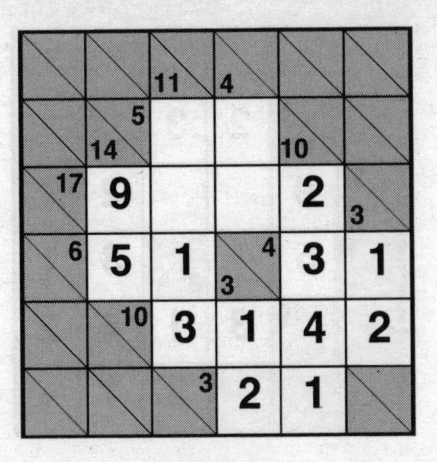

STEP FIVE

The cell across the top of puzzle adds up to **5**, which has only two combinations 1+4 and 2+3.

As 1 and 3 already appear on the cell running downwards marked with **11,** the left-hand square can only be a 2 or a 4.

However, if it was a 4 then the missing digit on the **11** down cell would have to be a 3, which is already represented. Therefore the **5** across cell must be 2+3 as on page 15:

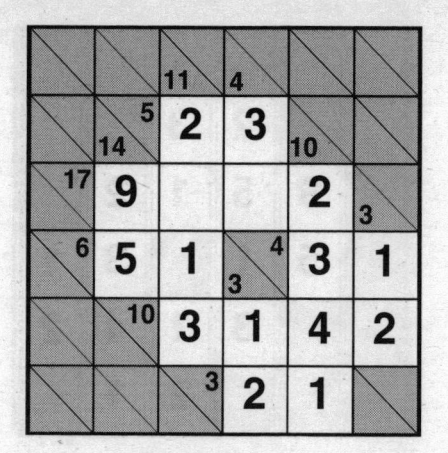

FINAL STEP

The puzzle is now easily solved by adding the 1 to make up the **4** down cell and a 5 to complete the **17** across/**11** down cell.

Kakuro puzzle grid with clues and entries:

- Clues: 11, 4, 5, 14, 10, 17, 3, 6, 4, 3, 10, 3
- Entries:
  - 2 3
  - 9 5 1 2
  - 5 1 3 1
  - 3 1 4 2
  - 2 1

LIST OF UNIQUE NUMBER COMBINATIONS

This list helps you identify where there is only one possibility to a cell's value – invaluable to helping you solve a Kakuro.

2 Cells
3 : 1,2
4 : 1,3
16: 9,7
17: 9,8

3 Cells
6 : 1,2,3
7 : 1,2,4
23: 6,8,9
24: 7,8,9

4 Cells
10: 1,2,3,4
11: 1,2,3,5
29: 5,7,8,9
30: 6,7,8,9

5 Cells
15: 1,2,3,4,5
16: 1,2,3,4,6
34: 4,6,7,8,9
35: 5,6,7,8,9

6 Cells
21: 1,2,3,4,5,6
22: 1,2,3,4,5,7
38: 3,5,6,7,8,9
39: 4,5,6,7,8,9

7 Cells
28: 1,2,3,4,5,6,7
29: 1,2,3,4,5,6,8
41: 2,4,5,6,7,8,9
42: 3,4,5,6,7,8,9

8 Cells
36: 1,2,3,4,5,6,7,8
37: 1,2,3,4,5,6,7,9
38: 1,2,3,4,5,6,8,9
39: 1,2,3,4,5,7,8,9
40: 1,2,3,4,6,7,8,9
41: 1,2,3,5,6,7,8,9
42: 1,2,4,5,6,7,8,9
43: 1,3,4,5,6,7,8,9
44: 2,3,4,5,6,7,8,9

9 Cells
45: 1,2,3,4,5,6,7,8,9

POCKET KAKURO FOR KIDS

1

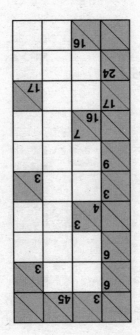

See page 68 for the solution

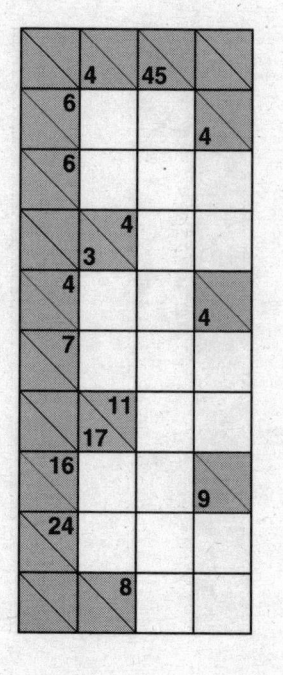

See page 68 for the solution

19

POCKET KAKURO FOR KIDS

3

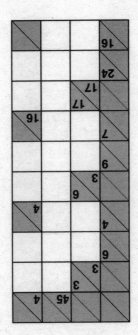

See page 69 for the solution

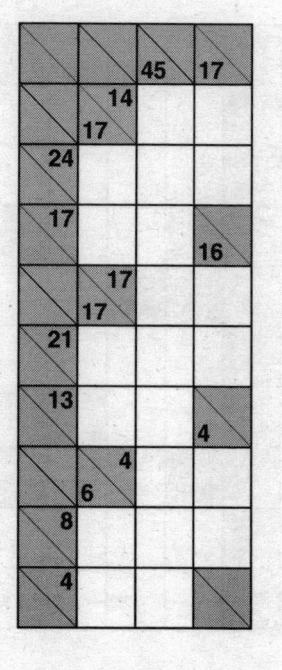

See page 69 for the solution

POCKET KAKURO FOR KIDS

5

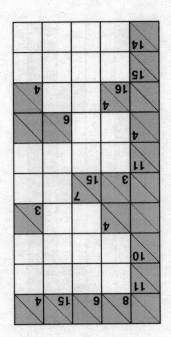

See page 70 for the solution

POCKET KAKURO FOR KIDS

6

See page 70 for the solution

POCKET KAKURO FOR KIDS

7

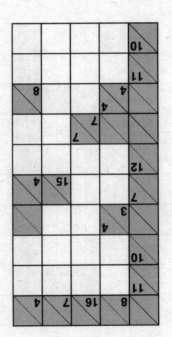

See page 71 for the solution

(24)

See page 71 for the solution

9

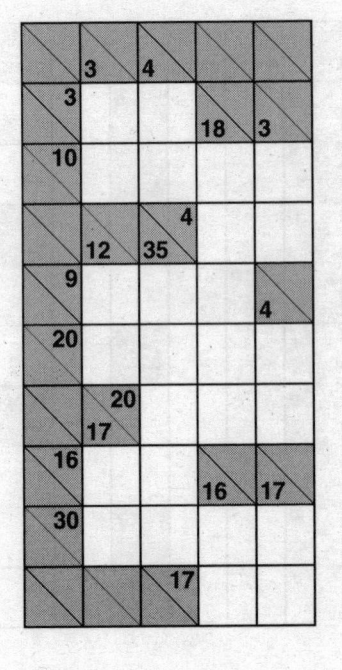

See page 72 for the solution

POCKET KAKURO FOR KIDS

10

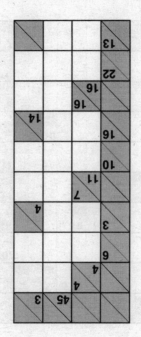

See page 72 for the solution

POCKET KAKURO FOR KIDS

11

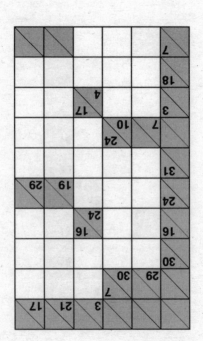

See page 73 for the solution

POCKET KAKURO FOR KIDS

12

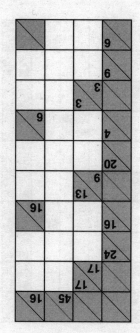

See page 73 for the solution

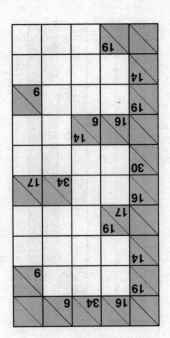

See page 74 for the solution

POCKET KAKURO FOR KIDS
14

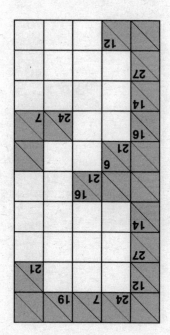

See page 74 for the solution

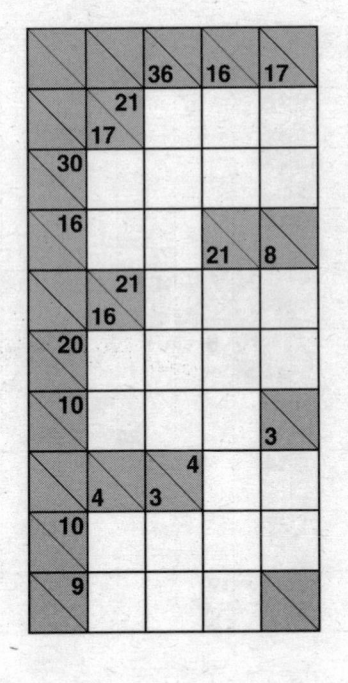

See page 75 for the solution

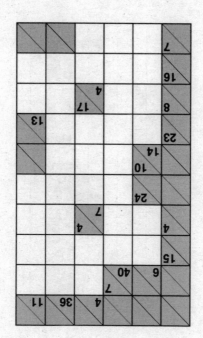

See page 75 for the solution

POCKET KAKURO FOR KIDS

17

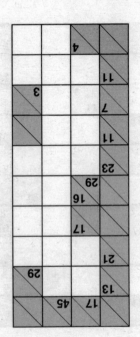

See page 76 for the solution

(34)

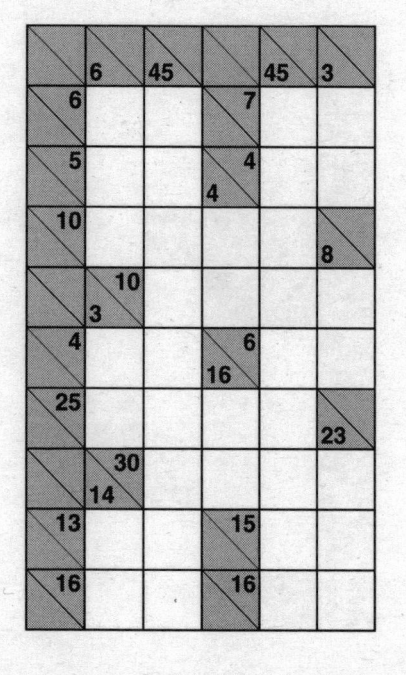

See page 76 for the solution

POCKET KAKURO FOR KIDS

19

See page 77 for the solution

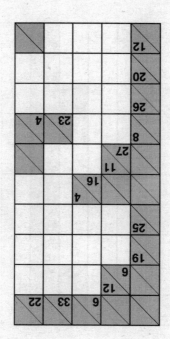

See page 77 for the solution

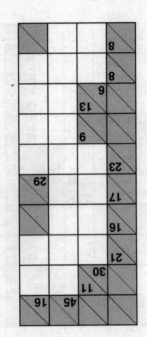

POCKET KAKURO FOR KIDS

21

See page 78 for the solution

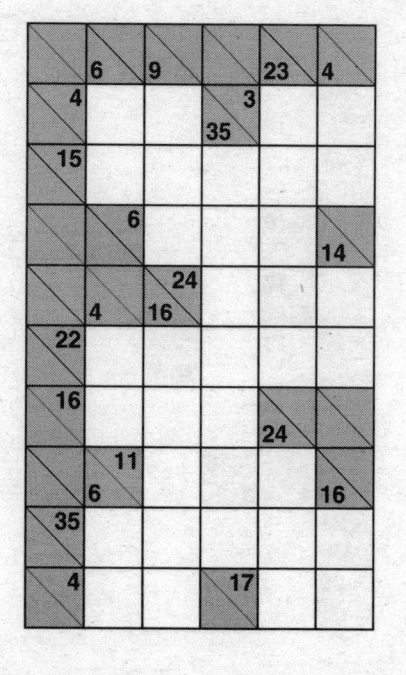

See page 78 for the solution

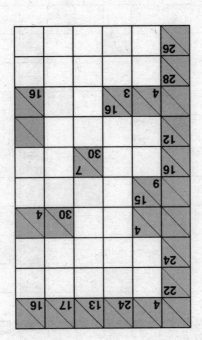

See page 79 for the solution

POCKET KAKURO FOR KIDS

24

See page 79 for the solution

See page 80 for the solution

See page 80 for the solution

POCKET KAKURO FOR KIDS
27

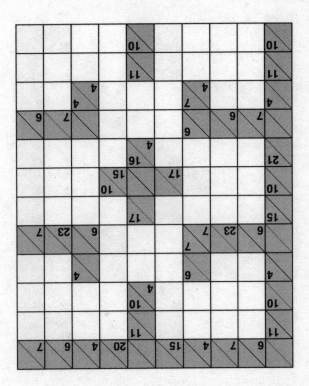

See page 81 for the solution

POCKET KAKURO FOR KIDS

28

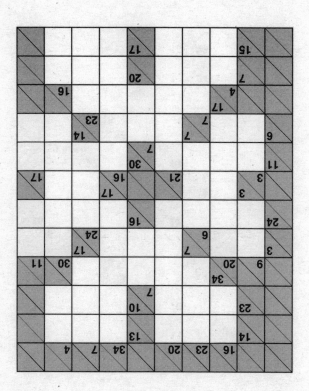

See page 81 for the solution

45

POCKET KAKURO FOR KIDS

29

See page 82 for the solution

See page 82 for the solution

POCKET KAKURO FOR KIDS

31

See page 83 for the solution

POCKET KAKURO FOR KIDS
32

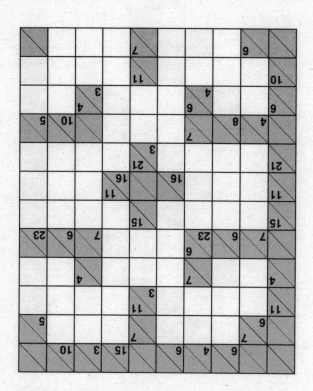

See page 83 for the solution.

See page 84 for the solution

POCKET KAKURO FOR KIDS

34

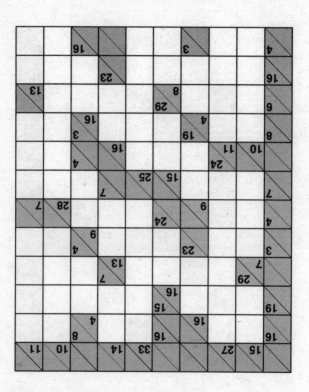

See page 84 for the solution

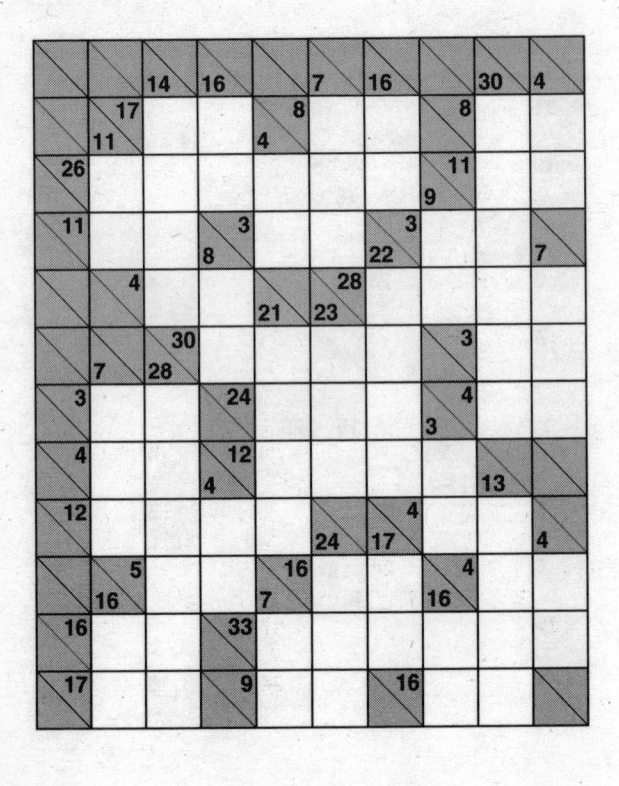

See page 85 for the solution

POCKET KAKURO FOR KIDS
36

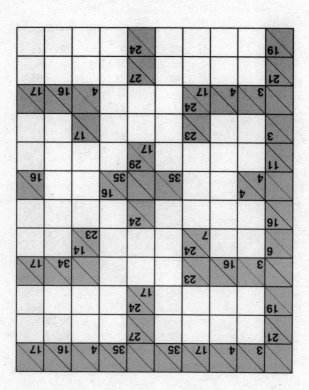

See page 85 for the solution

See page 86 for the solution

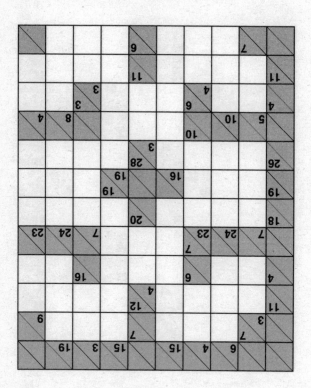

See page 86 for the solution

See page 87 for the solution

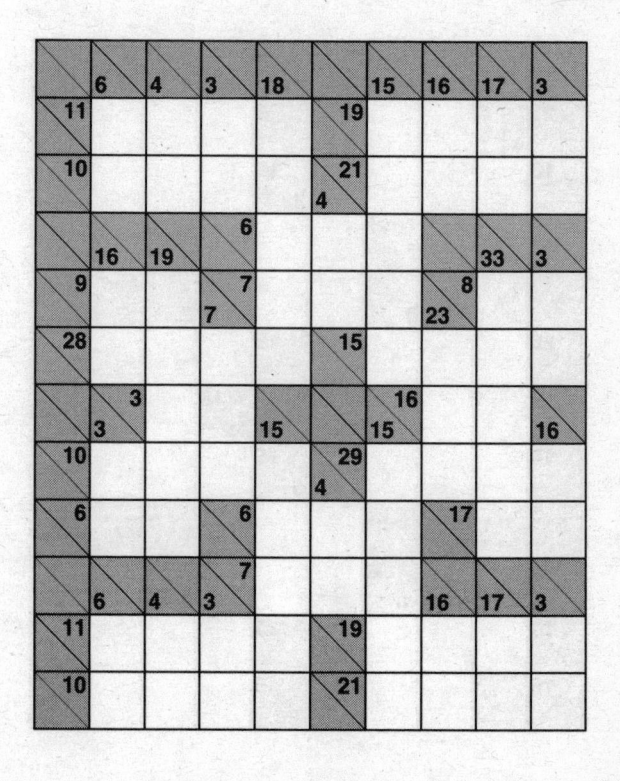

See page 87 for the solution

POCKET KAKURO FOR KIDS

41

See page 88 for the solution

POCKET KAKURO FOR KIDS

42

See page 88 for the solution

POCKET KAKURO FOR KIDS

43

See page 89 for the solution

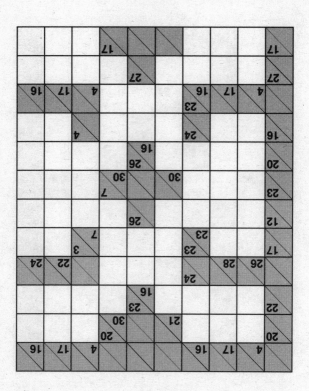

See page 89 for the solution

POCKET KAKURO FOR KIDS

45

See page 90 for the solution

See page 90 for the solution

POCKET KAKURO FOR KIDS

47

See page 91 for the solution

POCKET KAKURO FOR KIDS

48

See page 91 for the solution

POCKET KAKURO FOR KIDS

49

See page 92 for the solution

POCKET KAKURO FOR KIDS

50

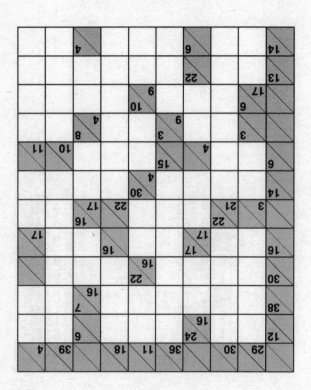

See page 92 for the solution

ANSWERS

1

1	5	
2	3	1
	1	2
1	2	
3	4	2
	6	1
9	8	
7	9	8
	7	9

2

1	5	
3	2	1
	1	3
1	3	
2	4	1
	8	3
9	7	
8	9	7
	6	2

ANSWERS

3

4

ANSWERS

5

5	1	2	3
3	2	4	1
	3	1	
		5	2
2	5	3	1
1	3		
	1	3	
9	2	1	3
7	4	2	1

6

		8	9
8	6	9	7
9	7		
	2	1	4
1	8	2	9
3	9	5	
		3	1
3	1	4	2
1	2		

7

5	1	2	3
3	2	4	1
	3	1	
1	6		
2	4	5	1
		4	3
	1	3	
3	2	1	5
1	4	2	3

8

1	5		5	3
2	1		2	1
3	2	1	4	
	4	3	1	2
9	8		3	1
7	9	8	6	
	7	9	8	6
2	6		9	8
1	3		7	9

ANSWERS

10

9

11

		2	4	1
5	7	1	8	9
7	9		9	7
9	8	7		
8	6	9	1	7
		8	7	9
2	1		9	8
1	7	3	2	5
4	2	1		

12

	8	9
8	9	7
9	7	
	6	7
6	5	9
3	1	
	2	1
1	3	5
2	4	

13

9	8	2	
7	4	1	2
	9	3	7
9	7		
8	6	7	9
		6	8
9	2	8	
7	1	4	2
	3	9	7

14

8	1	3	
9	4	6	8
7	2	1	4
		7	9
	4	2	
9	7		
4	1	7	2
8	6	9	4
	3	8	1

15

	4	9	8
8	6	7	9
9	7		
	9	5	7
9	8	2	1
7	2	1	
		3	1
3	1	4	2
1	2	6	

16

		1	4	2
5	4	3	2	1
1	3		1	3
	8	4	7	5
	6	1	3	
7	9	2	5	
1	7		8	9
2	1	3	6	4
4	2	1		

ANSWERS

17

8	5	
9	7	5
	8	9
	9	7
9	6	8
7	4	
5	2	
8	1	2
	3	1

18

1	5		5	2
3	2		3	1
2	1	3	4	
	4	1	2	3
1	3		1	5
2	6	9	8	
	9	7	6	8
5	8		9	6
9	7		7	9

19

8	7	9	6	
4	9	8	5	7
			7	9
		9	8	6
1	3	7	9	8
2	1	4		
4	9			
3	8	7	5	9
	7	6	9	8

20

	1	6	5
1	2	9	7
5	3	8	9
		3	1
	4	7	
6	2		
9	6	8	3
7	3	9	1
5	1	6	

ANSWERS

21

	4	7
7	5	9
9	7	
8	9	
6	8	9
	1	8
	6	7
1	2	5
5	3	

22

1	3		2	1
5	4	2	1	3
	2	1	3	
		7	9	8
1	2	5	8	6
3	4	9		
	1	3	7	
5	6	8	9	7
1	3		8	9

23

3	2	1	9	7
1	4	2	8	9
	1	3		
	5	7	2	1
7	9		4	3
2	3	6	1	
		7	9	
3	1	9	8	7
1	2	8	6	9

24

3	2	1		8	9		7	5	
1	4	2		5	7	9	6	8	
	1	3	2	4		7	8	9	
1	3		8	9			9	7	
5	6	8	9	7		7	4		
	9	7		7	9				
	5	7		7	9	8	4	5	
5	3			9	8		7	9	
1	2	3		8	6	7	9		
2	4	1	3	6		9	8	7	
3	1		1	5		8	6	9	

79

ANSWERS

9	8	7		9	2			4	9
8	6	9	7	4	1			6	8
7	9			9	8		1	3	
5	7	9			4	2	1		
		8	9	7	3			5	3
7	6			8	9	6		2	1
9	5			6	8	1	9		
	1	3	7			8	5	7	
	2	1		8	9			7	9
2	4			1	4	7	9	8	6
1	3		3	9			7	9	8

	4	2	1			4	2	1	
4	2	1	3			2	1	3	5
3	1			4	2	1		2	1
				2	1	3			
1	8	6	5			5	1	8	6
4	7	9					4	7	9
2	9	8	6			6	2	9	8
			4	2	1				
1	5			2	1	3		2	1
3	4	2	1			4	2	1	3
	2	1	3			2	1	3	

27

1	2	3	5			5	3	1	2
2	4	1	3			3	1	2	4
3	1		1	3	2		3	1	
			2	1	4				
1	8	2	4			6	1	8	2
3	6	1				3	6	1	
2	9	4	6		1	2	9	4	
			1	3	2				
1	3		2	1	4		1	3	
2	1	3	5		5	3	2	1	
4	2	1	3			3	1	4	2

28

	7	6	1		9	1	3	
	9	8	6		7	2	1	
		9	7	6	8	4		
1	2		2	1	4		8	9
8	9	3	4		6	7	1	2
	1	2				8	9	
2	3	1	5		6	9	7	8
1	5		1	2	4		5	9
	1	3	5	2	6			
	1	2	4		3	8	9	
	3	4	8		1	9	7	

29

6	8	9		8	9		5	7
8	9	7		5	7	9	8	6
9	7		2	1		7	9	8
	2	4	1	3	6		7	9
4	1	2	3		9	3		
2	3	1			1	3	2	
	3	9		3	2	1	4	
7	5		6	3	1	4	2	
8	9	7		1	2		7	9
6	8	9	7	4		7	9	8
9	7		9	8		9	8	6

30

	8	9	7		8	9	7	
1	6	8	9		6	8	9	7
3	9		8	9	7		8	9
			6	8	9			
1	8	2	4		4	1	8	2
3	6	1			3	6	1	
2	9	4	5		5	2	9	4
		8	9	7				
1	9		6	8	9		8	3
3	8	9	7		8	9	7	1
	6	8	9		6	8	9	

31

	8	9	7		8	9	7	
1	6	8	9		6	8	9	7
3	9		8	9	7		8	9
			6	8	9			
1	8	2	4		4	1	8	2
3	6	1				3	6	1
2	9	4	5		5	2	9	4
			8	9	7			
1	9		6	8	9		8	3
3	8	9	7		8	9	7	1
	6	8	9		6	8	9	

32

	2	1	4		1	2	4	
5	1	3	2		3	1	5	2
1	3		1	2	4		1	3
			3	1	2			
1	3	6	5		5	1	3	6
2	1	8				2	1	8
4	2	9	6		6	4	2	9
			1	2	4			
1	5		3	1	2		1	3
3	2	1	4		3	1	5	2
	1	3	2		1	2	4	

ANSWERS

33

4	2	1				1	4	2
8	4	3	2		8	3	9	4
3	1		3	1	2		3	1
			1	2	4			
1	6	8	9		9	1	6	8
2	8	9				2	8	9
4	9	7	2		8	4	9	7
			3	1	2			
1	3		1	2	4		1	3
4	2	1	5		3	1	4	2
2	1	3				3	2	1

34

7	9			7	9		3	5
8	4	7		4	5	3	2	1
	8	9	7	5		1	4	2
2	1		9	8	6		1	3
1	3		9	7	8			
4	2	1				1	2	4
		8	7	9			3	1
3	5		8	4	7		1	2
2	1	3		8	9	7	5	
4	2	1	6	3		9	8	6
1	3		2	1		9	7	

35

	8	9		1	7		7	1
2	1	7	3	4	9		8	3
9	2		1	2		1	2	
	3	1		7	8	9	4	
	7	9	8	6		1	2	
2	1		7	9	8		3	1
1	3		3	6	1	2		
4	5	1	2			1	3	
	2	3		7	9		1	3
7	9		6	9	8	7	2	1
9	8		1	8		9	7	

36

37

1	3	8	9		8	3	7	9	
2	1	9	7		6	1	9	8	
			6	8	9				
2	4		8	9	7		6	8	
1	6	4	5		5	6	4	9	
	3	1			9	7			
3	1	2	5		5	8	9	7	
1	2		6	8	9		8	9	
			8	9	7				
1	3	8	9		8	3	7	9	
2	1	9	7		6	1	9	8	

38

	9	7	8		9	8	6		
3	8	9	6		7	9	8	1	
1	6		9	8	6		9	2	
			7	9	8				
1	8	2	4		4	1	8	2	
3	6	1			3	6	1		
2	9	4	5		5	2	9	4	
			9	8	6				
2	7		7	9	8		9	2	
1	9	7	8		9	8	6	1	
	8	9	6		7	9	8		

39

	2	1	4		1	2	4	
2	1	3	5		3	1	6	2
1	3		1	3	2		9	7
		2	1	4				
1	8	6	3		5	1	8	6
2	9	8				2	9	8
4	7	9	6		8	4	7	9
		4	1	5				
3	1		3	2	1		2	1
2	5	3	1		2	1	5	3
	4	1	2		3	2	1	

40

3	1	9	8		9	3	8	1
1	2	7	6		7	1	9	2
			9	8	6			
7	4		7	9	8		6	3
9	8	4	5		4	6	2	1
	3	1				9	7	
3	1	2	4		5	8	9	7
1	2		9	8	6		8	9
			7	9	8			
3	1	9	8		9	3	8	1
1	2	7	6		7	1	9	2

41

2	3	1	5		1	7	9	2
4	1	2	3		3	9	8	1
			1	3	2			
7	2		2	1	4		6	2
9	8	4	7		5	6	3	1
	1	2				9	7	
2	3	1	4		5	8	9	7
1	5		1	3	2		8	9
			2	1	4			
2	3	1	5		1	7	9	2
4	1	2	3		3	9	8	1

42

	2	3	1		3	1	2	
3	4	1	2		1	2	4	3
1	5		5	2	4		5	1
			3	1	2			
1	8	2	4		5	1	8	2
2	9	4				2	9	4
3	6	1	4		5	3	6	1
			5	2	4			
3	1		3	1	2		1	3
4	2	3	1		3	1	2	4
	4	1	2		1	2	4	

43

1	4	2	7			9	3	7
3	2	1	9	7		8	6	9
	1	3		9	7	6	1	8
8	5			8	9		2	5
9	7			6	8	7		
6	3	1				9	7	4
		3	4	2			5	2
8	5		2	1			3	1
9	2	4	1	3		7	9	
7	3	1		5	3	8	6	9
4	1	2			1	9	8	7

44

9	2	1	7		8	1	7	9
8	1	3	9		6	3	9	8
			8	9	7			
7	6		6	8	9		7	9
9	8	6	5		4	8	6	5
	7	9				7	9	
7	9	8	5		5	9	8	7
9	5		8	9	7		5	9
			6	8	9			
9	2	1	7		8	1	7	9
8	1	3	9		6	3	9	8

ANSWERS

45

3	8	9				3	8	9
1	9	7	5		6	1	9	7
			8	7	9			
8	9		6	9	8		1	2
1	3	6	2		7	2	9	8
6	8	9				1	2	4
2	1	8	9		6	4	7	9
9	7		8	7	9		3	1
			6	9	8			
3	8	9	7		7	3	8	9
1	9	7				1	9	7

46

8	5			1	2		5	3
9	7		8	3	9		4	6
	8	6	9		3	1	2	4
1	6	2	7	3		3	1	2
3	9	7		1	7		3	1
		1	2		9	7		
5	3		1	9		9	7	3
2	4	1		7	9	8	6	1
1	2	3	5		7	6	1	
3	1		3	7	8		9	7
4	6		8	9			8	9

47

6	8	9	7		9	3	1	8
8	9	7	5		7	1	2	9
			8	9	6			
1	6		9	7	8		5	9
7	9	8	6		5	9	7	8
	7	9			8	9		
2	1	7	6		4	6	2	1
9	8		8	9	6		8	3
			9	7	8			
6	8	9	7		9	3	1	8
8	9	7	5		7	1	2	9

48

	2	9		2	9	1	3	7
8	1	2		4	8	6	7	9
9	7		6	1		5	9	
	6	9	8			9	8	
	5	7	9	8		6	3	
8	5		9	8	6		5	1
9	7		3	6	1	2		
	9	7			9	7	8	
	3	1		1	7		7	9
1	8	9	2	4		2	1	7
3	6	4	1	2		9	2	

ANSWERS

49

	2	9		2	9	1	3	7
8	1	2		4	8	6	7	9
9	7		6	1		5	9	
	6	9	8			9	8	
		5	7	9	8		6	3
8	5		9	8	6		5	1
9	7		3	6	1	2		
	9	7			9	7	8	
	3	1		1	7		7	9
1	8	9	2	4		2	1	7
3	6	4	1	2		9	2	

50

1	8	3	9		8	2	7	9
2	9	1	7		6	1	9	8
			8	9	7			
2	6		6	8	9		6	9
7	9	8	5		4	6	1	2
	7	9				9	7	
1	3	6	4		5	8	9	7
3	8		8	9	7		8	9
			6	8	9			
1	8	3	9		8	2	7	9
2	9	1	7		6	1	9	8